ques
and
marks

verses that ask punctuation that speaks

trushali prajapati

BlueRose ONE
Stories Matter
New Delhi • London

BLUEROSE PUBLISHERS
India | U.K.

Copyright © Trushali Prajapati 2024

All rights reserved by author. No part of this publication may be reproduced, stored in a retrieval system or transmitted in any form or by any means, electronic, mechanical, photocopying, recording or otherwise, without the prior permission of the author. Although every precaution has been taken to verify the accuracy of the information contained herein, the publisher assume no responsibility for any errors or omissions. No liability is assumed for damages that may result from the use of information contained within.

BlueRose Publishers takes no responsibility for any damages, losses, or liabilities that may arise from the use or misuse of the information, products, or services provided in this publication.

BlueRose ONE
Stories Matter
New Delhi • London

For permissions requests or inquiries regarding this publication, please contact:

BLUEROSE PUBLISHERS
www.BlueRoseONE.com
info@bluerosepublishers.com
+91 8882 898 898
+4407342408967

ISBN: 978-93-6452-608-1

Cover design: Tahira
Typesetting: Tanya Raj Upadhyay

First Edition: September 2024

questions and marks

for the life
conspiring
within me

questions and marks

yesterday was like a painful question
today is like a soothing answer
this book was written yesterday

questions and marks

contents

just questions.....................................1

questions and marks

it was pretty dark
in there with you
day in day out
i searched for the light
in your tunnel

in this loop of light,
was i recreating my
existence?

- the tunnel of thoughts

questions and marks

the thought of you leaving me
strewn my existence

was i the only one screaming in pain at losing myself in you?

questions and marks

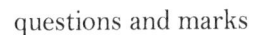

was i scared of losing you?
or
was i tired of falling in love again with someone new?

questions and marks

sometimes
you need to be
alone

alone with tangles
to find the right threads
in this path of life

alone with cluelessness,
to find the healing light
in the realm of your soul

but in this aloneness
do you mourn
for the sunsets
you used to gaze
in your lover's arms?

- threads

questions and marks

life in this world
is conflicting with
the one we think of
before we surrender our
souls to dreams

dreams guide us
to solace to chase
the deep falls

life before and after
each sleep keeps
changing our personas

do these personas lead us to touch the undiscovered parts of us?

- discovering myself after your love intrigued me

questions and marks

we were trying
trying to be lovers
in a world where
faith in love
was lost

we were trying
trying to be healers
in a world where
karma was lying
in hopes

was our love seeking its worth in these circles of faith and karma?

- destined to fall apart

questions and marks

is 'trance of dance' the great healer?

or

is 'to seize the fading memories tightly in your arms'

the great healer?

questions and marks

will you be looking

for me in the quiet

hours when i'm not there?

or

is it just me again

looking for you

in the loop of time

holding faded love

in whispered dreams and

in unuttered reality?

- unuttered

questions and marks

if you wanted to shred something apart then why didn't you shred

my fear of love
my fear of letting go
my fear of loneliness
my fear of trusting a soul?

why did you choose to shred the romantic tales i carried in my emotional baggage?

questions and marks

we were a half-finished conversation

in the chapter on fascinating words

we were disenchantment

in the world of lover's spells

we were a fleeting mirage

on the skyline of forgotten dreams

we were a fractured stardust

in the boundless midnight sky

- half-finished

questions and marks

confusion?
yes, it was confusion
on your face
when you asked me
to stay
with you all night
to talk
after a long
pause

talk about our
past love
talk about our
dwindle dreams
talk about our
voids of reality

but why did each
confused thought
of yours bring me
to my karmic disturbances?

questions and marks

does the universe gave
me a sign to be
in love with you?
or
does the universe gave
me a sign to entwine
with my past lover
from another life
where our kindred soul
can connect for a moment
in this lifetime
and separate with
a traumatic destiny?

questions and marks

you offered me your love,
the love you didn't have
in your heart for yourself

you offered me peace
when all you had
was a conflict of
emotions within that
skin of yours which
was imploding your soul

but how can you offer me something you don't have
within yourself?

questions and marks

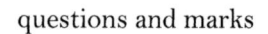

did every atom in this universe collide when we met?
or
was it just our bodies?

questions and marks

was someone else praying for you and infringing on my prayers?

- losing you over someone's prayer

questions and marks

for which new chapter, the old chapter has ended?

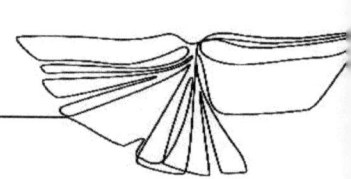

questions and marks

it was just a

three-letter word

for you but

for me it was an

emotion which tore

into countless words from

a book of lifetimes

- i leave you

questions and marks

are our minds full of noise?

the noise piled up in layers of your betrayal

questions and marks

if you would have told me that you are leaving
then i would have prepared myself with all the bursts
of sunshine.

questions and marks

i saw you in my dreams

begging me for forgiveness.

- reality isn't the same

questions and marks

half summer

when you seek a different place

half autumn

when my soul fade

half winter

when i wandered with grace

half spring

when my body serenade

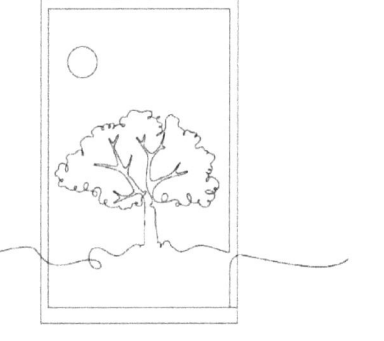

- half seasons

questions and marks

is our 'suitcase of life' so shallow as to crumble in pain?
or
is our 'lack of strength' a burden on our suitcases of life?

- later we divided our suitcases

questions and marks

why do we think about the realm of love when we are all alone on a path we have never been on before?

questions and marks

were you just a whisper in my fallacy prayers?
and
are the heavens still holding on to each wish of my whispers in silence?

- hoping for a new lover

questions and marks

i was dusted down from your present when your thoughts started aligning with someone else.

questions and marks

why now does it feel
like sudden blossoms
of cry to my soul
when all you were doing
is hurting me every
time with your
immense love?

questions and marks

i held my breath with a heavy heart

to utter one name of my lover

to my angels

in the middle of a stormy night

when i couldn't see the stars

guiding my path

i felt a whisper in the wind a vow in the rain

that the love would seek its way

leading me home

through the darkness of night

- angels

questions and marks

when you held
my hand to bind
me in the eternal
love of yours

i looked down
to our shadows
appearing from
the moonbeam

gradually your
shadow was fading
into darkness

were you drowning in your own utterly dark shadow?
or
did you come just for a snap of time to heal my
shadows?

questions and marks

did the moon forget to shine its lights on us?

or

did the moon forget to change its phases on us?

questions and marks

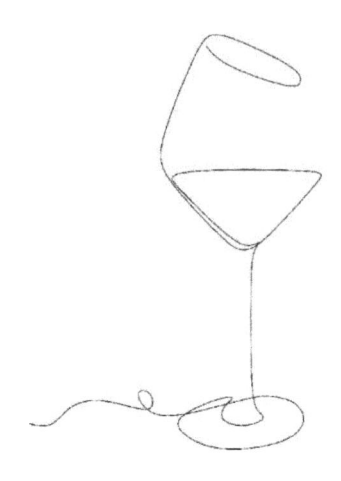

the empty glasses of yours
couldn't make me
drunken in love with you
anymore

questions and marks

you gave me your love

in breadcrumbs

like i begged you for survival

out of my hunger

i was starving for the feast

yet i nibbled each crumb

i was waiting for the love

that was whole

and not blunder

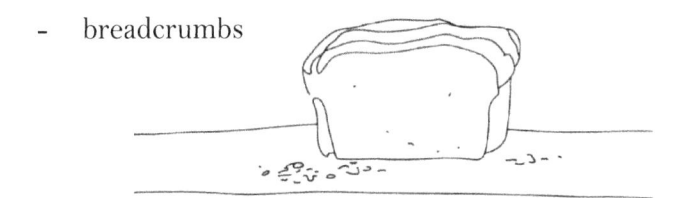

- breadcrumbs

questions and marks

will you stay close to my dreams if i give you my love?
or
will you sleep next to me for this lifetime if i disenchant my love?

- a troubled emotion

questions and marks

are you having scary dreams with calm feelings?
where the lost shadow dances on its own rhythm
but the heart scratches its wounds
or
are you having beautiful dreams with sudden blood rage?
where the flowers are circling its thorns
and the colours bursting its anger

- losing shadows with the thorns

questions and marks

were you thinking nothing when you decided to lose the path of freedom?

- love is freedom

questions and marks

my thoughts
felt dirty
when i met you
after years

that dirt was
over my brain
and in my heart
asking me to
leave you

but rather than
leaving i chose
to put myself
in the dirt

was that dirt worth leaving on the shine of my body?

questions and marks

i burned my memories
many times for you
and each time when
i remembered your name
i let the reflections of your
eyes drop from mine
with each passing reflection
my heart stitched its wounds

questions and marks

when you were leaving
i locked the doors
tightly from inside
so that no one could
ever unlock them

questions and marks

i ran to the window
to see you going
away from me
taking all the pieces
of mine within yourself

i realised that your
steps didn't even
bother to hold on
to me and your eyes
to see me for one last time

in there i was alone
playing with flames
turning my heart into ashes
walking on fire shedding
my brain within
but what stuck in my mind was why you didn't bother
yourself when i was locking the doors that night?

questions and marks

i always knew that you had vile eyes for me. remember when i persistently nudged you by questioning your eyes. remember when you said you love me. i said i feel your eyes would do something wrong to my harmony. now i wonder who shall i blame

the vile eyes
or
my bleeding feet going away from you?

questions and marks

you said while boarding the flight. i was the best thing that happened to you. you will always keep me in your heart. squeezed in your memories. in the safest suitcase which no one would know about.

am i supposed to be healing in your suitcase?

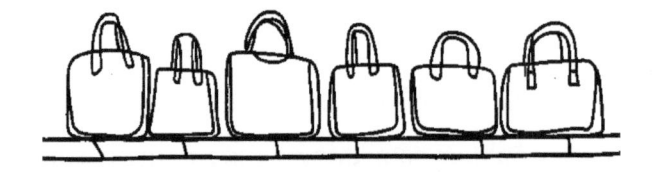

questions and marks

the reasons you gave me
were not enough for me
to let you go.

questions and marks

was your silence the answer to all my questions?

-   still waiting for the answers

questions and marks

why do we let this agony of uncoupling slide into our lives?
- decoupled souls

questions and marks

you bind my heart
with the needle you have
in your hand.

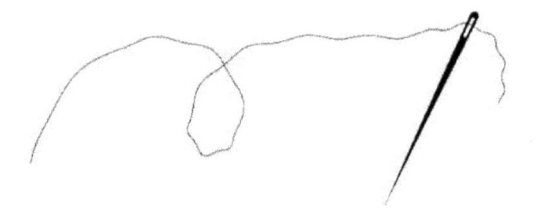

questions and marks

how you manipulate

your emotions for me?

how can you love me

in the night with grace and

leave me in the morning

with an empty space?

questions and marks

how many times i will keep sharpening my pencil to rewrite our stories?

questions and marks

why were you not gesturing to the music i was playing inside me?

- couldn't you feel that the music was for you

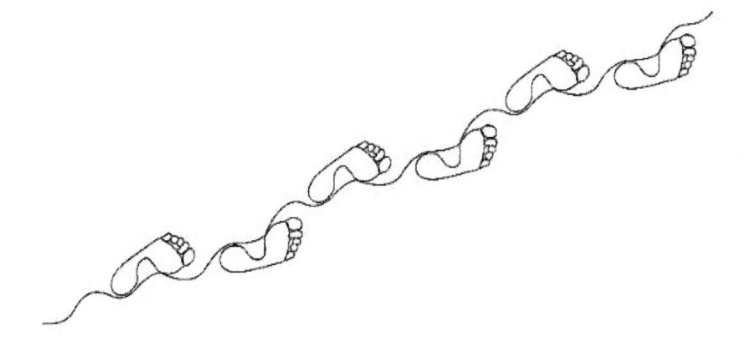

questions and marks

it was hard to unlearn the things i learned when i had you. the way you changed the side of the bed every night. those two tablespoons of sugar with your coffee every morning. the exact number of buttons you kept undone in your shirt before the office. the smell of the perfume you drowned yourself in. the way you took each step of yours: slowly. the way you looked at yourself in the mirror. the colours you liked. the music which soothes you. the list of movies you watched when you were in pain. the kind of open sky which brought you happiness. the way you breathe calmly. the way you carried all your thoughts within you. the way you twisted me several times on a beat which played inside our hearts. the way you gave me those sensations of your raged love.

now they keep floating in my mind, with echoes of a time when your presence was constant. unlearning is like trying to forget the warmth of the sun in a deadly summertime.

well, now it's not about wiping out the past but finding a way to exist in this world again and remarking on the footsteps without you in it.

questions and marks

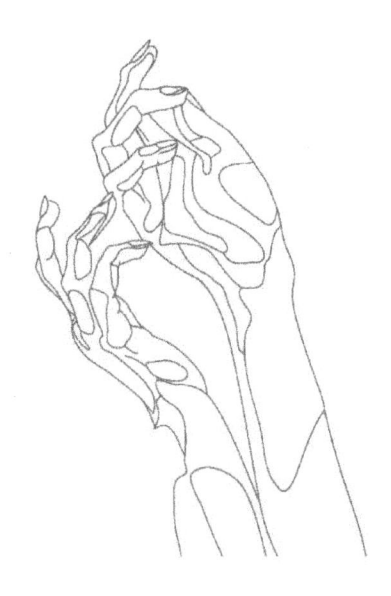

questions and marks

what is the one thing you will miss when you leave me?

- asking this when you are next to me holding my hand and the creases on our hands are flowing opposite to one another

questions and marks

questions and marks

there were those 30 seconds
where my heart paused
after seeing your face
for the first time in
those lonely crowds

there are these 30 years
where my heart shrank
sharing stories about you
and searching for your
lost smell in the
lonely crowds

- 30 seconds or 30 years of moving on from you?

questions and marks

was i meant to
hold my breath
when you choked
my neck with
unleash rope of
leftover feelings?

- yet i'm holding the marks of ropes around my neck

questions and marks

sometimes the tears soak away on their own, for the fear of losing myself for you. other times, my crumbled lungs can't hold my fearful drip of love for you.

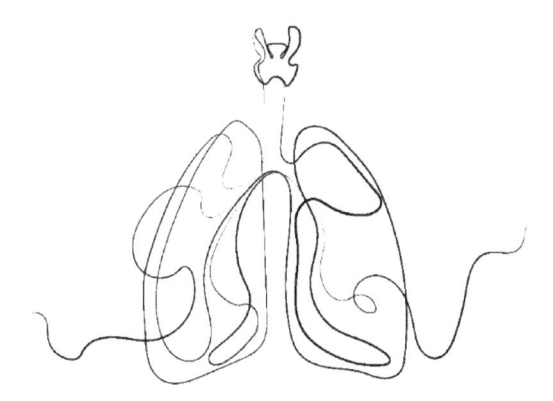

questions and marks

for letting you go away from my memory, i banished all my happy moments with you. for forgetting you, i forgotten myself. will each piece of my memory reflect down on those happy moments when the blossoms of my heart rise again?

questions and marks

the people in my surroundings force me to think about you.

questions and marks

i'm folding you in my thoughts, i keep folding your thoughts till i forget your face in the shadows of my eyes. with each instinct i get, those folds are becoming a burden on my long-lasting memories of agony now.

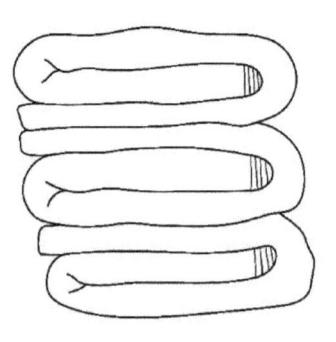

questions and marks

why did you pull yourself away from me
when we were a few moments away
from eternal closeness?

questions and marks

sometimes my thoughts
play up with me and
ask me amidst a night
when my body is twisting
along the bedsheets
was i a convenience for you?
or was i just a chapter in
your diary of inconveniences?

questions and marks

have you felt the
chaos within you
when a stranger
swings next to you
and dance in the
air of loneliness
with the melody
of love?
are you scared
of getting wrecked
by a stranger?

questions and marks

listen to the wind he said, like he was preparing me for the storm. does his blissful love always come with the intention of hurtful storms?

questions and marks

every loved one we have in this life
was the consequence of the sacred prayer
we did when we were souls yet you left
marking a question on our prayers

did we leave our faith in prayer behind
or did we forget to pray and lose everything
we love in this life?

questions and marks

in the desert, we lie, with a starry sky beholding our eyes, mesmerising its beauty, we make a memory of filling togetherness with our bodies. then why do we disobey that memory of lying our bodies on a sandy sky and twisting those stars who were gazing at our beauty of togetherness?

questions and marks

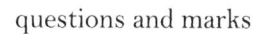

can i be free from the feeling of being locked in my lover's arms?

- a suffocating lover

questions and marks

was it the feeling of
separation that
squeezed my
tenderness
towards you?

questions and marks

you left saying you will never forget me, i was a beautiful thought for you. i was a sparkle in your smoked sun. when the reality was, you made up your mind to go miles away from me in your reminiscence and missed those thousands of suns to be with me.

questions and marks

is it about the burial we have at the end of lifelong love?
or
is it about beholding love with a chain of ruthless thoughts?

questions and marks

i will keep a picture of yours in the aroma of my eyes,
i will be cocooning our old memories in the subsets of
our love life.

questions and marks

will i be able to tell you someday
about all the days i have been
passing without you?

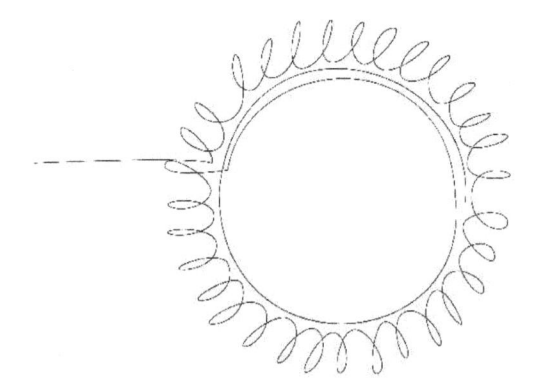

questions and marks

how many breaths did you take to consider me your soulmate?
and
how much moonlight faded my existence from your shadow?

- beginning and end of everything

questions and marks

with each passing day i realise
how badly i got played
by you.

questions and marks

does love look like withdrawing emotions?

questions and marks

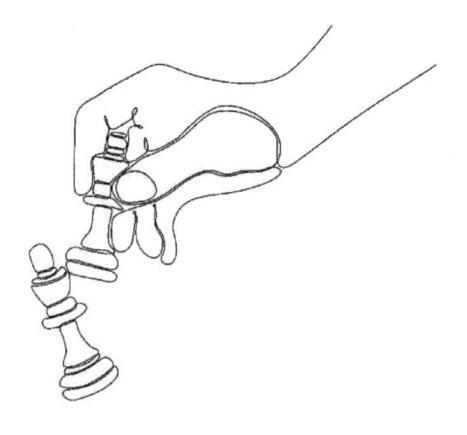

questions and marks

why does it feel like a sudden hurt
in my soul when you left,
when all you were doing
was hurting me each time
with your immense love?

questions and marks

when is the right time to inhale the portion of love?
and
when is the right time to exhale the karmic illusions?
- on love, separation, and karma

questions and marks

the thing is

i forget the

difference between

love and lust

when you left.

questions and marks

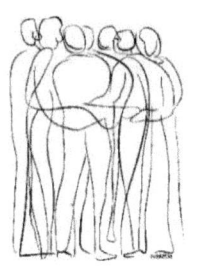

why i allowed
you to heal
a part of me
which no one
ever tried to heal?

questions and marks

i am still loyal to you
creating our memorials in
every corner of our house
even when you are no
longer with me

- memorials

questions and marks

i have creased millions
of light paths to be in
the darkness with you
along the time i witnessed
the plague crippling over
the shine i have within me

- plaque

questions and marks

i was feeling empty
while writing you
down in words

never knew that
the words will
take your place
as metaphors
of your unpassionate
warmth in my life

-       alone with words

questions and marks

long hold you took

when i asked you

to stay

yet i asked you again

thinking that

my re-question

can change

your mind

- yet you left, leaving behind the traces of your presence

questions and marks

the fall i had

forced me to

destroyed

the person i was

born with

- 'the fall' given by you

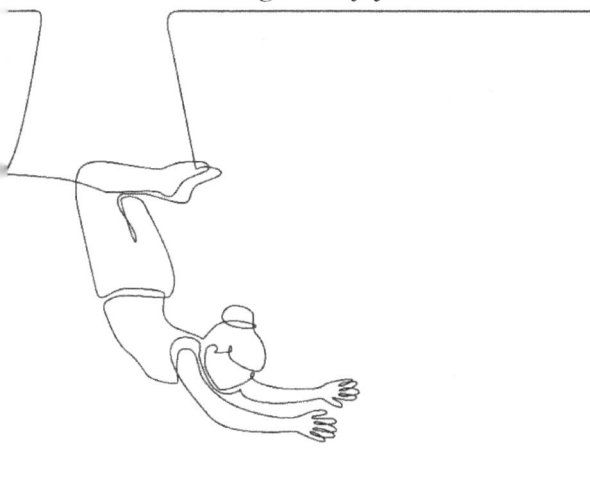

questions and marks

are you accountable for the miseries you gave me?

questions and marks

you were screaming among the strange souls. seemed like someone tortured you in the walls. you were shattering the mirrors of my reflections, holding me tight yet couldn't give confessions. you detoured your emotions of unsurety for so long that the cyclonic breath of yours flew my soul no more. yet we danced in shadows where the spark couldn't reach, your whispers echoed on a deserted beach. each word of yours shattered my dream. i tried to stitch the pieces of my broken dreams. but did not realise that your heart was a fortress, guided by the tortured sins.

- tortured

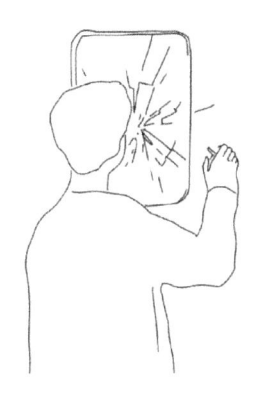

questions and marks

you are here for

the fragile body

i come with

and not for

the fragile heart

i hold in

questions and marks

i chose you

you chose everyone else

questions and marks

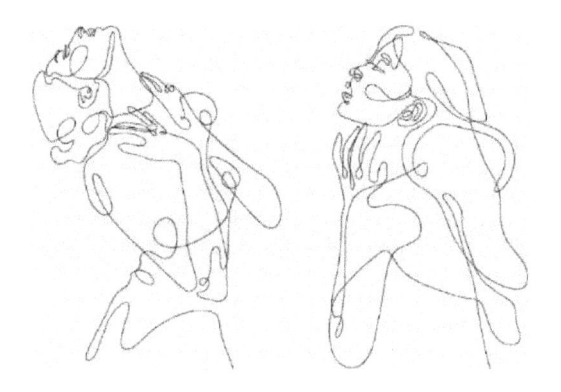

questions and marks

your stand was on
kissing those fragile lips
of mine and to touch me
on the places i haven't
touched myself

your marks are still
on the places
you missed touching

- a soul needs healing

questions and marks

can a 'sorry' undo the scars?

questions and marks

did you burn my letters when you met her?
the fragments of inks, now lost in the air
every word once admired, now turned to ash
did you burn my letters, the oldest pieces of mine?
the burden of words, you wished to shed
past love of yours, now consumed by the flames

- wake of new love

questions and marks

was it obvious that you wanted to leave?

and

was i holding you tight because i was scared of losing you?

questions and marks

you wanted me to forgive you
for something you weren't even sorry for

questions and marks

the idea of being
close to him
made me drown
in my thoughts

the thoughts which
has a nameless
journey in the
delusional stories
visiting me at
each passing
phase of a warm
summer dawn

yet, i kept the thoughts alive through my words

- i forgave him for his sins but my words couldn't forget him

questions and marks

i keep asking myself
before every sleep
what if you come back
i keep playing with
millions of scenarios
in my head of your arrival
and they all start with
how will i greet you if
you come back

- come back

questions and marks

at a certain point in this life,
why do we have to let
all our questions fade away
deep in our memories?

- a lover who wants to heal

questions and marks

a year passed today. the scars on the tiniest pieces of my destructed soul started healing. i let your memories shatter down in the lane of the crying sky. i let my feelings fly over a dark cloud. each passing breath of mine asked me tangled questions and you were not there to untangle them. your voice started fading in the dunes of flowing sand. i kept screaming your name in the endless horizons with strange hands. i felt hollowness within. you were miles away to hear my perilous voice. and at some point my voice paralysed touching your thoughts. a year has passed, and i'm still waiting for my voice to be heard.

questions and marks

can we be friends even if you see love in my eyes and gestures?

- a lover who wants to compromise just heard

questions and marks

will i stop choosing words over emotions if i start healing?

- a poet who doesn't want to stop healing through words

questions and marks

questions and marks

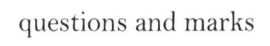

how can you bid me farewell without a beautiful closing line of the play you were leading?

questions and marks

why does my heart keep wandering that you have someone else in your life?

questions and marks

why i keep chasing your hanging love?

questions and marks

how can you be so unkind to me yet want me for eternal lifetimes?

questions and marks

how many times do you think about me in a day?

-	i'm rusted with your thoughts

questions and marks

remember when you used to call me at midnight with your lame questions on your intolerant life. questions to be a better man. questions on how you will win your football match tomorrow. questions on the universe not being on your side, and always choosing the worst for you. questions on forcefully walking down the path which is solely created by you. questions on your past which you are pulling away the strings from. questions where you felt healed but emptied inside. questions which made you inconsistent. questions on your existence. questions on your broken stories of lost lovers. questions of you being lonely all your life, left alone by familiar faces. questions on being destroyed several times yet holding each breath. questions on losing yourself within divine powers yet feel greedy. questions on evolving even when you feel caged with your tortured thoughts. questions on not supporting yourself and seeking support from elsewhere. questions on feeling incomplete when you see yourself in the mirror. questions on waiting for love when you can't even love yourself. questions on leaving people whom you loved the most.

although i knew your questions, i was unafraid to love you. yet you did what you were supposed to do. unheard all the answers given by me. little did i know that i would find myself asking the same questions when you shattered my existence into sobbing tears.

questions and marks

questions and marks

are you pretending to be okay without me?

questions and marks

the closed curtains have witnessed many stories when you used to visit me no longer.
the terrible sense of your touch with dread. unfaithful conversions with myself facing mirrors for hours and hours. and the flood of tears. anxieties and panic attacks. restlessness. sadness. screaming in pain. wailing on walls. stains of blood. ripping hair. darkness for several moons. no wind rush. desperation to hold you. a long list of undone work. as my curtains fragmented into millions of short stories without you.

- the closed curtains

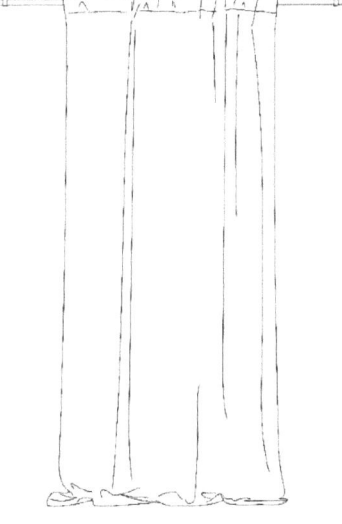

questions and marks

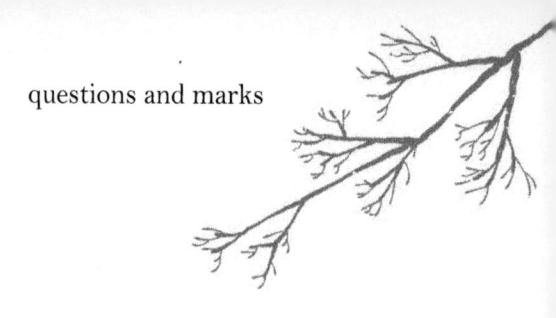

i am an autumn tree

waiting for the golden rays

to show their miracle on me

questions and marks

why i persist in a
restless pattern
of chasing you,
following your
thousand signals,
when all i wanted
was just one sign
to hold you till
infinity?

- mixed signals

questions and marks

i was silently seeking your love
from the distance but this time when
you came close to my vulnerable life
i broke down into tears i have been
waiting to pass since i saw you
for the very first time

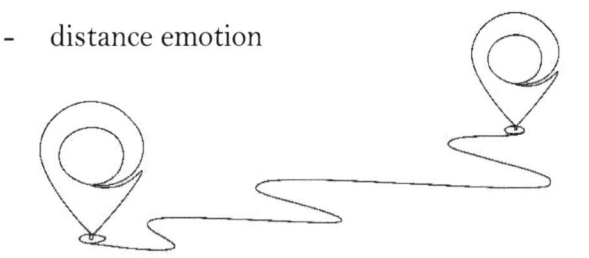

- distance emotion

questions and marks

why am i still mourning
when i have everything with me,
just not you?

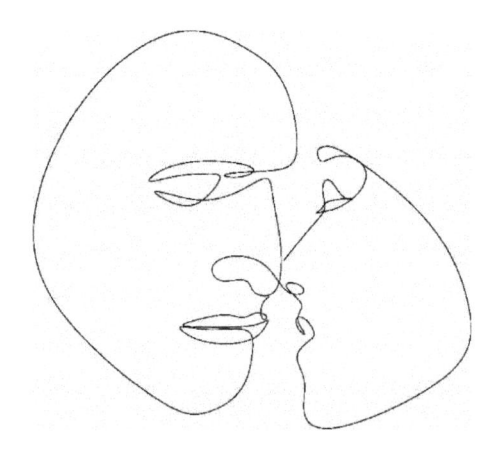

questions and marks

questions and marks

couldn't you stay for a while even after hearing my forlorn whispers?

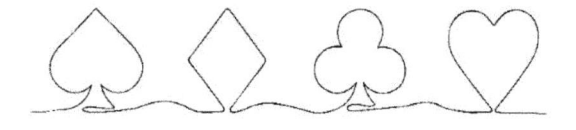

questions and marks

questions and marks

i kept visiting the foreteller

to know our story, our destiny,

but each time, her visions

and her twisted cards

left my heart in cold mystical lands

questions and marks

why did i meet you when i can't have you?

-	a lover who can't clasp another lover

questions and marks

you were a piece of thoughts
in my wisdom of words
you were a pinch of ocean
in my articulate feelings
you are now a murmur
in the silence that remains
until i rebirth myself

- rebirth

questions and marks

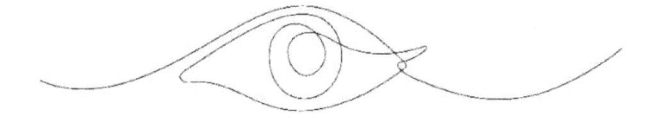

i can't see myself in pieces of you

questions and marks

i have been waiting for my answers
dancing to endless music
tapping my feet harshly
on every beat
looking at the closed doors
of your chambers
seeking for a small light
waiting and waiting
till you come and bind my pieces
with your answers
but scared from inside
for you not having answers
leaving me again in rust and dust
so can you please at least tell me that you have all my answers?
so can you please promise to answer me when the right time comes?

questions and marks

why couldn't i work on myself
after working on you for years and years?
pouring all my force into your ambitions
yet you left me empty, surfacing my fears
abandoning my own heart's silent tears

questions and marks

maybe years down the line
i will figure out why the universe
sent you in my chaotic life
but for now let me clean
the stains of you

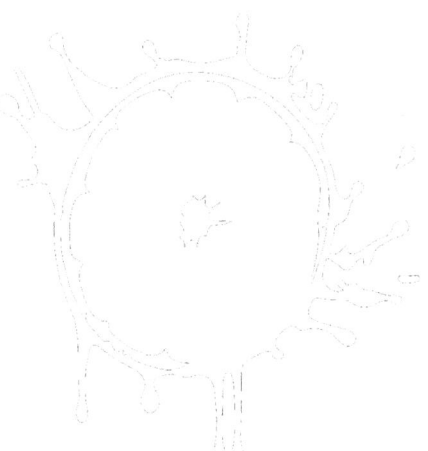

questions and marks

i was a comfort for you. you used to visit my holiness when you had no place to go. you drank me when you were drowning in your well of foul water. you lingered in my fragile bed of emotions when you wanted to pass your few seconds in faking pleasure. you were hungry for the way i used to caress each tissue you were born with. the tiny shivers of yours always chained a path to me. you wanted someone to walk with you in case you will start feeling lonely in the loophole of darkness within your brain. you had me when you needed a corner for your soul. a corner where i grew a valley of flowers on the cracks of your walls and flavoured the fragrances from palettes of life. but you left sucking down the shine through my skin. cracked each part of naiveness within me, turned it down like your cracked wall, when you realised that you could gamble the comfort from someone else too.
- cracked comfort

questions and marks

can we repeat those unholy romances so that i can feel myself again?

questions and marks

i know you loved me
but there is a part of me
which doesn't love myself

-       a self-lover

questions and marks

no longer i
believe in past lovers
coming back home

- a small home created by us with the curtains of omens

questions and marks

honey, i'm home, you used to say. half opening the door with a piece of cake in your hand. so that i don't question your lateness. you started giving all the irrelevant excuses by yourself. someday you were stuck in traffic. other day you had plenty of work at the office. someday you went for drinks rituals with your colleagues. other day you were buying me gifts. someday your car got flat. other day you bumped into an old friend. someday you stop at mid-road to seek a beautiful sun. other day the flood held you miles away from home.

but now, the door stays closed. the excuses are soundless. the cake is missing from your hands, and so are you. there is a void in the house without your stories. i find myself craving for the days when you would rush in with a smile, a piece of cake, and a tale to tell. in the silence, i knew that the excuses were never about the lateness. they were about sharing my day with your new lover.

questions and marks

was it love?

or

were you luring me into another trauma called love?

questions and marks

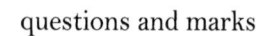

why i keep slipping down into the zones of fragility in the name of love?

questions and marks

i was so much rooted for you that i never realised my feet were lingering in the sand of your diluted emotion.

questions and marks

i knew that the time
has come to let you go
the second my heart
started holding on to
each breathes when you
were close to me

the clock of our
long-lasting love
has stopped
i was pushing back
the hand of second
to ghost the time
out for you

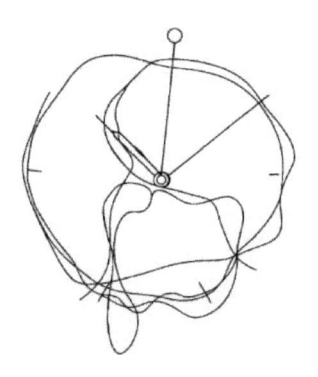

- but the cycle of my heart couldn't hold onto you

questions and marks

you left a persona
of mine created
by you

turning me from a
brutally bold to
weakest of all
changing my flow from
wild river of thoughts to
stagnant water of delusions

turning my intuitions into damages
damages made with love

turning my worth into passive sadness
sadness of deep wounds

- just turning me in spirals of a blackhole where
  i couldn't even find myself

questions and marks

i never turned back after you puppeteer me into your fabricated stories, yet i kept waiting for you till i saw the last star of your vigilant soul.

questions and marks

am i on my own now?

the only thought which kept whispering to my mind after you left

questions and marks

why did you break the bridge between our hearts?

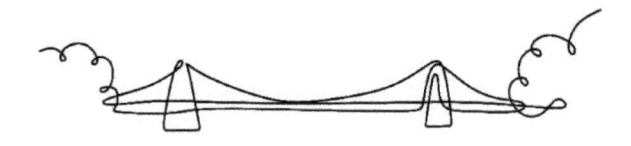

questions and marks

the roots of our love weren't tangled so hard.

-     some tangles are good

unrushed milk is turning into high tides.

unglazed television is up beating the warmth of moonbeams on a summer night.

unhurried footsteps are whispering with the birds flying up in the rainy skies.

unforgettable jazz relives with the heartfelt cwtch in the middle of a luminant moonlight.

- this is the ache i endured each passing day without you

questions and marks

you were a conundrum

which is

untouched

and

unhealed

questions and marks

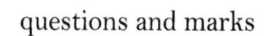

why did i burn down my vivaciousness into ashes of lost feelings when you left?

questions and marks

our broken story will stick with you even if you walk down the path of recreating yourself with her. you will show her the pinch of me you took with yourself. you might stir the echoes of the emotions in her which i once stirred in you. you might ask her to touch you in the places i have touched you. you might want to hear my words from her mouth when you make love with her. you might want to taste the food i serve when you dine with her. you might want to see my face when you wake up in the middle of the night holding her tight. you might find yourself seeking my name on your phone screen as if its presence on your screen were a familiar comfort while calling her. you might scream my name asking for coffee even though you know i'm nowhere near to you. you might miss the texture of my hand when you are walking down in a clear sunny sky with her. you might give her the shades of blue assuming that she will look exactly like me after wearing them. you might search for the smile i used to give after a long day at work. you might be complimenting her the same way you used to compliment me, losing into an illusion that she is my reflection. everything you do on this path will end up finding me in her.

perhaps someday you will tell her that you can't love her because she is not the echo of my soul.

questions and marks

like the wind flows

i wanted to

flow with

you

questions and marks

were we just a battleground where we kept pondering our hard illusions on each other?

questions and marks

i might pour my heart out
with a glass of whiskey
by seeing the glare of me
in your eyes and the calmness
you have within them by
holding my reflections
as i know i will never get to
see them next to me when
each dawn's light finds me
stirring from within

questions and marks

a part of me is hiding the force i feel around you and a part of me is plucking the dead flowers from shallow dreams to seek you

questions and marks

i have started sharing
the portions of life
with monochromes
as you ruined
the meanings of
colours for me

- monochromes

questions and marks

i kept saying that i didn't care. yet i used to fly on the roads where i met you for the very first time. thinking that maybe someday our paths will clash. and we will hold each other again the same way dawn's first light meets the waves of the ocean.

questions and marks

there were these bubbles of dreams i created with you

questions and marks

i kept my doors open for you
several nights after you left
in case one night you want
to rush down my lane

questions and marks

it was your decision to betray us. you stepped on the path which leads you towards her. you had me in your mind and her on your bed. you satisfied your emotional hunger with her and yet came back to me. a dozen thoughts crossed my bed that night. the rain turned into a flood, and the drought came with dead alarms, yet you cast the spell upon me for the path you chose for yourself.

questions and marks

you wanted to stay
yet you drained my house of hearts
you were a puzzle
yet i allowed you to pluck me from
the garden i have been
watering since i was a child

- puzzle

i used to receive friendly reminders. when you were sketching the entire game plan on how to mark those deep wounds on my back and burn my wings of romance.

the dreams of your existence fading from mine, the harsh way you started connecting to my lips. the way our evening shows were telecasting in two different rooms, the way you started turning your back on me while sleeping, the way you stopped watering my growth, the way one meal started serving on two different plates, the way you stopped sharing your office stories, the way you keep scrolling down your social media on your phone and intentionally ignore the small talks with me, the way you started taking those long walks all by yourself. the way you lied from those gibberish words, the way my towel used to hang up on my skin even if you were around. the way the moonlight kept poking from our slightly open curtains showing misery. the way my eyes were digging a well to hold on to each drop of tear when you marked those wounds along my wings.

from the depth of several souls i always knew what you were up to. yet i paid no attention to my instincts and dwelled on the path of my breakage on my own.

- the way

questions and marks

you were a warrior to me
a soulful warrior
who embedded
lightness into
darkness

- some people come into your life to pilferage
  the light you have within

questions and marks

suddenly it feels like i'm orbiting the marathons of unattended emotions.

questions and marks

questions and marks

why don't i care about having marks of yours on my holy parts?

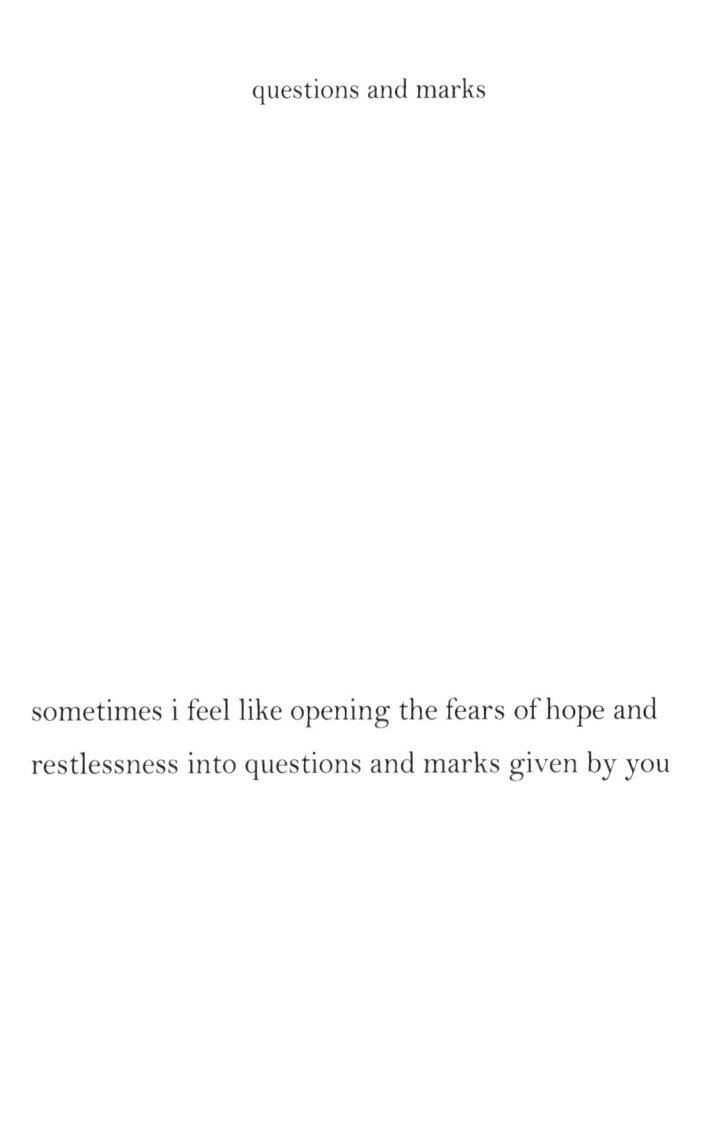

questions and marks

sometimes i feel like opening the fears of hope and restlessness into questions and marks given by you

about the book

*questions and marks are
the stack of questions
asked by a lost lover from the
edge of her broken window and
the stack of immeasurable marks
given to her tortured soul*

*she counted her marks and
questioned herself in
agony
suffering
loss and
self-doubts*

*this is a journey of questioning
and counting on the most
fragile moments of hanging love
and healing through words*

questions and marks

from the author

i ran to the window on a rainy summer night when he was leaving. i saw him walking away from me. his last words were, "i have to let you go". i ran and screamed inside the shattered glass of the window. hoping to see him back. that night my questions started flying up in a dark sky. i turned and twisted the birth and rebirth in just one life. holding on to each question of mine. i came to my readers. thank you for reading my pain. thank you for sticking with me on this journey of my abandoned questions. i promise i will listen to all your questions too someday. maybe that day i will be able to answer you, which your lover couldn't answer. for now, i share with you the strength i have within. so you can dance with the universe. healing your questions and marks.

- *breathe with me*

about the author

trushali prajapati is a management consultant and a poet. she published her first poetry collection while working towards her management consulting role. since childhood, trushali chose to play with words after seeing her mother read and write. trushali's words are fragmented into questions and marks on losing breaths, love, life and her true self. she tried to heal herself while travelling to some beautiful cities. touching the cities from her heart, she started writing in their most beautiful parks. she always believed that going away from your home country could heal you, and she became a healer through her words. you can always drop her a 'question' on her instagram (@trushaaali). she is enchanting her life into a story, inspiring all around her to be more of a storyteller.